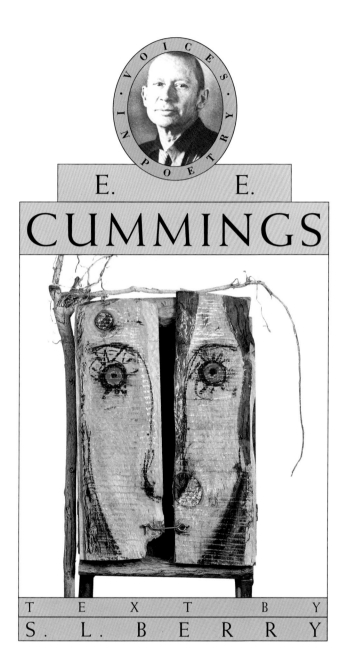

VOICES · IN · POETRY

E.   E.
CUMMINGS

T E X T   B Y
S. L. B E R R Y

A R T W O R K   B Y

S T A S Y S   E I D R I G E V I C I U S

CREATIVE EDUCATION

you shall above all things be glad and young.

For if you're young,whatever life you wear

it will become you;and if you are glad

whatever's living will yourself become.

Girlboys may nothing more than boygirls need:

i can entirely her only love

whose any mystery makes every man's

flesh put space on;and his mind take off time

that you should ever think,may god forbid

and(in his mercy)your true lover spare:

for that way knowledge lies,the foetal grave

called progress,and negation's dead undoom.

I'd rather learn from one bird how to sing

than teach ten thousand stars how not to dance

From *Collected Poems*

5

"If a poet is anybody, he is somebody to whom things made matter very little—somebody who is obsessed by Making."

E. E. Cummings made this observation in the introduction to *is Five*. He was, himself, a poet obsessed by Making. Combining an artist's sense of visual composition with a writer's sense of verbal manipulation, he created poems that looked and sounded entirely new.

Cummings was an odd combination of avant-garde modernist and old-fashioned lyricist. A staunch believer in the rights of the individual, he wrote biting, satirical poems that were critical of the dehumanizing aspects of industry and government. Yet he was also an unabashed romantic, writing lovely, lyrical poems that celebrated nature and the human spirit. And despite their disjointed appearance, many of his poems were written in traditional rhymed and metered verse forms.

Foregoing commercial success for artistic experimentation, Cummings created poems so unique that they permanently altered poetry's artistic boundaries. In the process, he earned a reputation as one of America's most daring and innovative poets.

E. E. Cummings, poet and artist.

l(a

le
af
fa

ll

s)
one
l

iness

From *95 Poems*

*E*dward Estlin Cummings was born on October 14, 1894, in Cambridge, Massachusetts, the first of two children born to Edward and Rebecca Cummings. Estlin's sister, Elizabeth, was born in 1896.

Edward Cummings, Senior, was the first professor of sociology at Harvard University; he later became the minister of one of Boston's most respected Unitarian churches. He was an excellent writer and speaker, inciting in Estlin a fascination with language and word play. He was also a skilled carpenter and taught his son to use his hands as well as his mind.

Rebecca Cummings was a warm, happy woman who loved spending time with her children. She sang to them and played games with them. She also taught both of them to read. An avid diary-keeper and amateur poet, she introduced Estlin to the pleasure of writing while he was still quite young, recording his diary entries for him, then urging him to add illustrations.

Estlin grew up in a spacious, sunny house that his father told him he had built "in order to have you in."

His neighborhood was full of children, most of them the offspring of Harvard professors. Estlin and his friends roamed the nearby woods, playing cops and robbers or blindman's buff. In the winter, they skated on a local pond; in the summer, they played baseball on vacant lots. And regardless of the season, when they wanted to rest, they retreated to Estlin's treehouse, a roomy, sturdy place with a porch and a small working stove on which they toasted apples and popped corn.

Each summer, the Cummings family spent several weeks at Joy Farm, their rural residence near Silver Lake, New Hampshire. Estlin spent his days there exploring woods and pastures, while learning how to use a compass and to identify wildlife. His evenings were spent with books—a family tradition was to have one member read aloud every evening.

As an adult, Cummings acknowledged the tremendous impact his parents had had on him, stating that it had been "my joyous fate and my supreme good fortune" to belong to such a family.

Edward Cummings, Sr., with Estlin and Elizabeth.

in Just-

spring   when the world is mud-

luscious the little

lame balloonman

whistles   far   and wee

and eddieandbill come

running from marbles and

piracies and it's

spring

when the world is puddle-wonderful

the queer

old balloonman whistles

far   and   wee

and bettyandisbel come dancing

from hop-scotch and jump-rope and

it's

spring

and

     the

          goat-footed

balloonMan   whistles

far

and

wee

From CHANSONS INNOCENTES [Innocent Songs]
Tulips section, *Tulips and Chimneys*

*B*ecause learning and literature were so valued in his family, Cummings grew up surrounded by books. Among his favorites were *The Arabian Nights, The Odyssey,* and *King Arthur and His Knights.* His family's evening readings also introduced him to Charles Dickens's *David Copperfield* and Robert Louis Stevenson's *Treasure Island.*

At the age of eight, Estlin began attending private school. When he transferred to a nearby public school two years later, his reading skills were so advanced that he was promoted to the seventh grade. He was only twelve years old when he enrolled as a freshman in the Cambridge Latin School, a college preparatory program housed in a building next to Cambridge High School.

Estlin was a good student, though not outstanding. As required, he studied Latin, French, and Greek, besides reading books from Harvard's recommended reading list. He also wrote for the school's monthly *Cambridge Review,* eventually serving as its literary editor in his senior year. But neither his own writing nor the works he selected for the *Review* hinted at the literary maverick Cummings would become.

Cambridge Latin School.

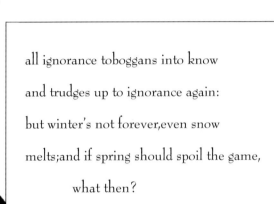

all ignorance toboggans into know

and trudges up to ignorance again:

but winter's not forever,even snow

melts;and if spring should spoil the game,

what then?

all history's a winter sport or three:

but were it five,i'd still insist that all

history is too small for even me;

for me and you,exceedingly too small.

Swoop(shrill collective myth)into thy grave

merely to toil the scale to shrillerness

per every madge and mabel dick and dave

—tomorrow is our permanent address

and there they'll scarcely find us(if they do,

we'll move away still further:into now

From 1 x 1

COLLEGE

*I*n 1911 Cummings graduated from the Latin School and headed down the street to Harvard University. Academically, Cummings spent his time deepening his understanding of languages. He concentrated on Greek studies, but he also took courses in Spanish and German. He broadened his literary background by studying Shakespeare and lyric poetry.

As important as his academic courses were to him, Cummings's leisure-time activities were even more so. He loved circuses and ballets, operas and ragtime piano bars, amusement parks and symphonies. He also loved the company of young women. Pale and blond with hazel eyes and high cheek bones, Cummings had good looks, a quick smile, and an enthusiasm for life that attracted women to him. He was an excellent dancer and an incorrigible romantic. On more than one Sunday morning, his mother had to hurriedly clean the hairpins out of the back seat of the family car before her husband drove it to church.

As his social life got livelier, Cummings's artistic interests expanded. He fell in with a group of freethinkers and became acquainted with the Cubists' experiments in painting. A self-taught painter in both oil and watercolor, Cummings began to try his hand at abstracts. His interest in Cubism soon spilled over into his creative writing, and it was during this time that Cummings first began rearranging sentences and spacing words on a page in an attempt to achieve specific visual and verbal effects.

His new pursuits put Cummings in conflict with his more conservative father, who couldn't understand his son's desire for personal and artistic experimentation. Refusing to recognize Estlin as an adult, Cummings senior often treated him as a stubborn, wayward child. The result was a frustrating series of arguments and shouting matches.

By the time Cummings graduated from Harvard in 1916, he was ready to leave Cambridge for good.

the Cambridge ladies who live in furnished souls

are unbeautiful and have comfortable minds

(also, with the church's protestant blessings

daughters, unscented shapeless spirited)

they believe in Christ and Longfellow, both dead,

are invariably interested in so many things—

at the present writing one still finds

delighted fingers knitting for the is it Poles?

perhaps.   While permanent faces coyly bandy

scandal of Mrs. N and Professor D

. . . . the Cambridge ladies do not care, above

Cambridge if sometimes in its box of

sky lavender and cornerless, the

moon rattles like a fragment of angry candy

From SONNETS—REALITIES
Chimneys section, *Tulips and Chimneys*

WORLD WAR I

*I*n January of 1917, Cummings moved to Greenwich Village, New York City, where he'd landed a job at a publishing company. Bored with his daily routine, however, he soon quit. He planned to live life on his own terms, he told his parents, as a painter and a poet.

But the world interfered with his plans. On April 6, 1917, the United States formally entered World War I. Faced with the likelihood of being drafted, Cummings enlisted as a driver in the Norton-Harjes Ambulance Service. Though a pacifist, Cummings had no desire to go to prison for his beliefs; ambulance service seemed the least objectionable way to take part in a war he didn't believe in. Ironically, he ended up in prison anyway.

Cummings and Slater Brown, a friend from Harvard who also had enlisted in the ambulance service, were sent to France. When they reached their unit in the French countryside, their disdain for military discipline and for following orders led to their arrests as suspected German spies. They were imprisoned in a former seminary in a small French village, along with forty other men from various countries.

The prisoners spent their days in one large room where they slept, talked, read, and otherwise tried to cope with boredom and fear. The poor diet and lack of hygiene took its toll as well, and illnesses were common. Already slender, Cummings became rail thin; a vitamin deficiency led to a skin rash and depression.

After three months, Cummings was released, thanks to contacts his father had in Washington. (Brown was released a short while later.) Though it was a miserable ordeal, Cummings's imprisonment did serve a purpose: It became the subject of his first book, *The Enormous Room,* a prose account of his experiences published in 1922.

World War I doughboys.

I lift my eyes. I am standing in a tiny oblong space. A sort of court. All around, two-story wooden barracks. Little crude staircases lead up to doors heavily chained and immensely padlocked. More like ladders than stairs. Curious hewn windows, smaller in proportion than the slits in a doll's house. Are these faces behind the slits? The doors bulge incessantly under the shock of bodies hurled against them from within. The whole dirty *nouveau* business about to crumble.

Glance one.

Glance two: directly before me. A wall with many bars fixed across one minute opening. At the opening a dozen, fifteen, grins. Upon the bars hands, scraggy and bluishly white. Through the bars stretching of lean arms, incessant stretchings. The grins leap at the window, hands belonging to them catch hold, arms belonging to the hands stretch in my direction . . . an instant; then new grins leap from behind and knock off the first grins which go down with a fragile crashing like glass smashed: hands wither and break, arms streak out of sight, sucked inward.

From *The Enormous Room*

EMERGENCE

*D*espite his efforts to avoid army service, Cummings was drafted in May 1918. But by the time his basic training ended, so had the war. He then spent six months at an army camp in Massachusetts, chafing at the restrictiveness of military life.

Military service was not a positive experience, but it did give Cummings time to think. By the time he returned to New York City in 1919, he had formulated a basic set of values that shaped the way he lived for the rest of his life. The twenty-four-year-old had concluded that, as an artist and a poet, he valued the acts of painting and writing more than the resulting pictures and poems. On a social level, he preferred the company of nonconformists and people who were uncorrupted by privilege and power. And personally, he balked at any attempt to restrict his freedom to think, say, and do as he pleased; he had no intention of conforming to anyone else's idea of acceptable standards.

Many of these values were reflected in Cummings's writing. For example, the most famous of his stylistic devices—his use of the lowercase "i" as a personal pronoun—came about as a result of his admiration for the handyman who took care of the Cummings family cottage on Silver Lake, near Joy Farm. Poorly educated, he wrote letters to Cummings's father in which he referred to himself as "i"; the humbleness this suggested was very appealing to Cummings.

i sing of Olaf glad and big

whose warmest heart recoiled at war:

a conscientious object-or

his wellbeloved colonel(trig

westpointer most succintly bred)

took erring Olaf soon in hand;

but—though an host of overjoyed

noncoms(first knocking on the head

him)do through icy waters roll

that helplessness which others stroke

with brushes recently employed

anent this muddy toiletbowl,

while kindred intellects evoke

allegiance per blunt instruments—

Olaf(being to all intents

(continued)

a corpse and wanting any rag

upon what God unto him gave)

responds, without getting annoyed

"I will not kiss your f.ing flag"

straightway the silver bird looked grave

(departing hurriedly to shave)

but—though all kinds of officers

(a yearning nation's blueeyed pride)

their passive prey did kick and curse

until for wear their clarion

voices and boots were much the worse,

and egged the firstclassprivates on

his rectum wickedly to tease

by means of skilfully applied

bayonets roasted hot with heat—

Olaf(upon what were once knees)

does almost ceaselessly repeat

"there is some s. I will not eat"

our president,being of which

assertions duly notified

threw the yellowsonofabitch

into a dungeon, where he died

Christ(of His mercy infinite)

i pray to see;and Olaf, too

preponderatingly because

unless statistics lie he was

more brave than me:more blond than you.

From *W[ViVa]*

*C*ummings published his first book of poetry, *Tulips and Chimneys*, in 1923. Containing a variety of his experimental verses, the book got mixed reviews. Though some critics were confused and put off by what they perceived as Cummings's eccentric style, others appreciated his attempts to infuse poetry with the modernist spirit. "It is extraordinarily good," wrote one reviewer. "It contains, in its own individual and unprecedented style, as beautiful poems as have been written by any present-day poet in the English language."

Besides challenging the critics, Cummings upset several printers who were reluctant to reproduce his poems as written. Because of the peculiar spacing, punctuation, capitalization, and syntax that appeared in Cummings's work, some printers made "corrections" when they set the type, re-establishing what they saw as proper grammar and structure. This infuriated Cummings. He finally solved the problem by finding one printer—S. A. Jacobs—who understood what he was trying to do artistically. Together, Cummings and Jacobs oversaw the production of more than a dozen poetry books and prose collections that the poet published between 1925 and 1960.

"noise no 13," an oil painting by E. E. Cummings, 1925

Buffalo Bill's

defunct

    who used to

      ride a watersmooth-silver

          stallion

and break onetwothreefourfive pigeonsjustlikethat

                Jesus

he was a handsome man

          and what i want to know is

how do you like your blueeyed boy

Mister Death

From *PORTRAITS*
Tulips section
Tulips and Chimneys

*O*ne of the saddest periods in Cummings's life occurred shortly after his discharge from the army. He fell in love with Elaine Thayer, the wife of a close friend. The Thayers lived in separate residences, and Scofield Thayer was openly disdainful of conventional marriage. He actually encouraged Cummings to become involved with Elaine.

Cummings and Elaine had a daughter, Nancy, in 1919, but though the Thayers divorced when Nancy was a year old, Cummings continued to play the role of Elaine's boyfriend; he was unable to accept the roles of husband and father. He continued to spend his days in his Greenwich Village studio writing and painting, and his nights on the town carousing.

When Nancy was four, Elaine finally convinced Cummings to marry her. But marriage didn't change Cummings's behavior. When Elaine's sister unexpectedly died soon after the wedding, Cummings virtually ignored his wife as she struggled to make funeral arrangements and settle her sister's estate. In disgust, Elaine took Nancy and headed for Europe. On the outbound ship she fell in love with a wealthy Irishman.

When Elaine asked for a divorce, the shock jolted Cummings back to reality. He realized his behavior had driven his wife and child away. But Elaine would not change her mind, and after months of tortured negotiations, she got her divorce. She remarried and moved with her new husband to Ireland, taking Nancy with her.

Nancy grew up believing Scofield Thayer was her father. It wasn't until she was in her mid-twenties that she learned the truth and made contact with Cummings. Though happy to see her, Cummings denied Nancy the close relationship she wanted. He preferred to love her as he had for most of her life—from a distance.

it really must

be Nice, never to

have no imagination)or never

never to wonder about guys you used to(and them

slim hot queens with dam next to nothing

on)tangoing

(while a feller tries

to hold down the fifty bucks per

job with one foot and rock a

cradle with the other)it Must be

nice never to have no doubts about why you

put the ring

on(and watching her

face grow old and tired to which

you're married and hands get red washing

things and dishes)and to never, never really wonder i

mean about the smell

of babies and how you

know the dam rent's going to and everything and

                never, never

Never to stand at no window

because i can't sleep(smoking sawdust

cigarettes in the

middle of the night

From *is 5*

In 1926 Cummings's parents were involved in an accident while on the way to Joy Farm. Driving in a snowstorm at night, Edward Cummings failed to stop at a railroad crossing, and his car was rammed by an oncoming train. He died instantly. Rebecca Cummings survived, thanks in part to the bedside support she received from her two children.

Though Cummings and his father had often been at odds over the years, there was a genuine bond of love between them. Before his death, Edward Cummings had made peace with his son, and the two men had established a warm friendship. But it wasn't until thirteen years after Edward's death that Cummings was able to adequately and eloquently express his love for his father in the poem "my father moved through dooms of love."

Writing that poem, Cummings later remarked, was the beginning for him of a new sense of moral responsibility as a poet.

Joy Farm, Silver Lake, N. H.

my father moved through dooms of love

through sames of am through haves of give,

singing each morning out of each night

my father moved through depths of height

this motionless forgetful where

turned at his glance to shining here;

that if(so timid air is firm)

under his eyes would stir and squirm

newly as from unburied which

floats the first who,his april touch

drove sleeping selves to swarm their fates

woke dreamers to their ghostly roots

and should some why completely weep

my father's fingers brought her sleep:

vainly no smallest voice might cry

for he could feel the mountains grow.

Lifting the valleys of the sea

my father moved through griefs of joy;

praising a forehead called the moon

singing desire into begin

joy was his song and joy so pure

a heart of star by him could steer

and pure so now and now so yes

the wrists of twilight would rejoice

keen as midsummer's keen beyond

conceiving mind of sun will stand,

so strictly(over utmost him

so hugely)stood my father's dream

his flesh was flesh his blood was blood:

no hungry man but wished him food;

no cripple wouldn't creep one mile

uphill to only see him smile.

(continued)

Scorning the pomp of must and shall

my father moved through dooms of feel;

his anger was as right as rain

his pity was as green as grain

septembering arms of year extend

less humbly wealth to foe and friend

than he to foolish and to wise

offered immeasurable is

proudly and(by octobering flame

beckoned)as earth will downward climb,

so naked for immortal work

his shoulders marched against the dark

his sorrow was as true as bread:

no liar looked him in the head;

if every friend became his foe

he'd laugh and build a world with snow.

My father moved through theys of we,

singing each new leaf out of each tree

(and every child was sure that spring

danced when she heard my father sing)

then let men kill which cannot share,

let blood and flesh be mud and mire,

scheming imagine,passion willed,

freedom a drug that's bought and sold

giving to steal and cruel kind,

a heart to fear,to doubt a mind,

to differ a disease of same,

conform the pinnacle of am

though dull were all we taste as bright,

bitter all utterly things sweet,

maggoty minus and dumb death

all we inherit,all bequeath

and nothing quite so least as truth

—i say though hate were why men breathe—

because my father lived his soul

love is the whole and more than all

From *50 Poems*

L   O   V   E

$\mathcal{F}$ollowing his short-lived marriage to Elaine, Cummings became involved in a seven-year relationship with a vivacious woman named Anne Barton. When Cummings married Anne in 1929, his mother gave him Joy Farm as a wedding present. But Anne's inability to be faithful, as well as his inability to make enough money to support the free-spending life-style she loved, ultimately led to their divorce in 1932. She immediately married a wealthy surgeon.

Soon after his divorce from Anne, Cummings met and fell in love with Marion Morehouse, an elegant and stunningly beautiful model and actress. Her sophistication, combined with an appreciation for simple things—walks in the park, dinner in small Italian restaurants, fresh flowers—made her alluring to Cummings. And her organizational and business skills made her indispensable to him professionally. Though they never formally married, Cummings introduced Marion as his wife for the rest of his life.

somewhere i have never travelled,gladly beyond

any experience,your eyes have their silence:

in your most frail gesture are things which enclose me,

or which i cannot touch because they are too near

your slightest look easily will unclose me

though i have closed myself as fingers,

you open always petal by petal myself as Spring opens

(touching skillfully,mysteriously)her first rose

or if your wish be to close me,i and

my life will shut very beautifully,suddenly,

as when the heart of this flower imagines

the snow carefully everywhere descending;

(continued)

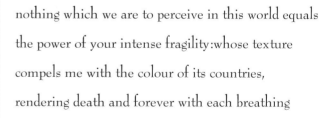

nothing which we are to perceive in this world equals

the power of your intense fragility:whose texture

compels me with the colour of its countries,

rendering death and forever with each breathing

(i do not know what it is about you that closes

and opens;only something in me understands

the voice of your eyes is deeper than all roses)

nobody,not even the rain,has such small hands

From *W[ViVa]*

By the time he was in his thirties, Cummings had become an accomplished, though not particularly distinctive, visual artist. He had exhibited his abstract paintings in a few large New York exhibitions, done commissioned works for friends and family members, and occasionally contributed ink drawings to magazines.

Gradually, Cummings's infatuation with abstract art gave way to an interest in realism. The result was the 1931 publication of *CIOPW*, a book filled with drawings and paintings of people and places. (The title stood for charcoal, ink, oil, pencil, and watercolor.) Later that same year, he mounted a one-man exhibit of similar works in a New York gallery. A *New York Times* critic remarked that "Cummings the painter, like Cummings the poet, is first of all an intelligent experimenter."

Though his work as a visual artist never earned him the same recognition and appreciation as his poetry, Cummings continued to draw and paint throughout the rest of his life.

"View From My Room," a pencil drawing by Cummings depicting the scene outside a Paris hotel.

Picasso

you give us Things

which

bulge:grunting lungs pumped full of sharp thick mind

you make us shrill

presents always

shut in the sumptuous screech of

simplicity

(out of the

black unbunged

Something gushes vaguely a squeak of planes

or

between squeals of

Nothing grabbed with circular shrieking tightness

solid screams whisper.)

Lumberman of The Distinct

your brain's

axe only chops hugest inherent

Trees of Ego,from

whose living and biggest

bodies lopped

of every

prettiness

you hew form truly

From PORTRAITS
XLI Poems

POLITICAL CHANGE

As a young man, Cummings had supported left-wing politics and pacifism, but as he grew older he became increasingly conservative. His political transformation began in 1931 when he toured the Soviet Union. There he found a political system that he felt stifled individual expression and repressed individual rights. For Cummings, this was intolerable. "I loathed it," he later said of Soviet Communism.

Eventually, Cummings came to detest not only Communism, but any political philosophy that he perceived as compromising individual rights for the benefit of the state. He became bitterly opposed to liberal American politics, which cost him some of his friends in New York literary and art circles.

However, Cummings did retain his outlook on pacifism throughout his life. Many of his most satirical poems deal with his opposition to war, the blind patriotism he believed causes it, and the wastefulness of lives that results.

The Red Square in Moscow, 1932: Troops and workers celebrate the fifteenth anniversary of the Bolshevist Revolution.

when serpents bargain for the right to squirm

and the sun strikes to gain a living wage—

when thorns regard their roses with alarm

and rainbows are insured against old age

when every thrush may sing no new moon in

if all screech-owls have not okayed his voice

—and any wave signs on the dotted line

or else an ocean is compelled to close

when the oak begs permission of the birch

to make an acorn—valleys accuse their

mountains of having altitude—and march

denounces april as a saboteur

then we'll believe in that incredible

unanimal mankind(and not until)

From *XAIPE*

*I*n 1947 Cummings's mother died at the age of eighty-seven after suffering a stroke. At her funeral, Cummings's sister, Elizabeth, read a poem he'd written for their mother several years earlier, entitled "if there are any heavens."

The loss of his mother was an emotional blow to Cummings—and a financial one. For years, Rebecca Cummings had subsidized her son's unorthodox lifestyle by sending him a monthly allowance. Now living expenses and the upkeep of his New York apartment and of Joy Farm quickly used up the money he'd inherited from his mother's estate.

In need of a new source of income, Cummings began touring the country giving poetry readings. These tours, in addition to paying well, gave him a chance to introduce his poetry to a variety of audiences, which improved sales of his books. He quickly established a reputation as one of America's finest public readers.

At the height of his popularity as a reader, Cummings was in his early sixties. By then he hated the rigorous travel schedules his tours demanded, but he loved the attention he attracted. Seated behind a table, Cummings alternated reading prose passages and poems, skillfully revealing the beauty and humor in his works.

After attending a Cummings reading in Boston in 1957, a reviewer for *Harper's* magazine wrote: "The big crowd loved him. He read slowly, meaningfully, lovingly—lingering on each syllable without losing for an instant the drive and surge of his poems. . . . Though it is banal to say over and over that poetry is something to be *heard*, one must say it—and say it again—to describe Cummings's impact on his listeners."

Cummings at his New York City apartment.

i f there are any heavens my mother will(all

      by herself)have

one. It will not be a pansy heaven nor

a fragile heaven of lilies-of-the-valley but

it will be a heaven of blackred roses

my father will be(deep like a rose

tall like a rose)

standing near my

(swaying over her

silent)

with eyes which are really petals and see

nothing with the face of a poet really which

is a flower and not a face with

hands

which whisper

This is my beloved my

                (suddenly in sunlight

he will bow,

& the whole garden will bow)

       From *W[ViVa]*

43

FINAL READING

*C*ummings spent the afternoon of September 2, 1962, splitting firewood in the barn on Joy Farm, as he'd done so many times since boyhood. When he finished, he went back to the house to clean up for dinner. On his way upstairs, he collapsed. Marion telephoned for help, but there was nothing anyone could do. Cummings had had a brain hemorrhage. At 1:15 A.M. on September 3, he died at the age of sixty-seven. A few days later, in a small private ceremony, the poet was buried in a Boston cemetery, not far from the graves of his father and mother.

Ten years earlier, Cummings had introduced the last lecture in a series with these lines, which in retrospect seemed to sum up his life:

"Ecstasy and anguish, being and becoming; the immortality of the creative imagination and the indomitability of the human spirit—these are the subjects of my final poetry reading."

when god lets my body be

From each brave eye shall sprout a tree
fruit that dangles therefrom

the purpled world will dance upon
Between my lips which did sing

a rose shall beget the spring
that maidens whom passion wastes

will lay between their little breasts
My strong fingers beneath the snow

Into strenuous birds shall go
my love walking in the grass

their wings will touch with her face
and all the while shall my heart be

With the bulge and nuzzle of the sea

From SONGS, Tulips section
Tulips and Chimneys

ACKNOWLEDGMENTS

Edited by S. L. Berry and Nancy Loewen
Photo research by Ann Schwab
Design assistant: Mindy Belter

PHOTO CREDITS

Nancy T. Andrews
Cambridge Historical Commission
The Everett Collection
The Granger Collection
The Houghton Library, Harvard College Library
Marion Morehouse
Photo Researchers, Inc.
Photo research contributed by Kathleen Reidy.

SELECTED WORKS BY E. E. CUMMINGS

POETRY
Tulips and Chimneys, 1923
XLI Poems, 1925
is 5, 1926
W[ViVa], 1931
No thanks, 1935
Collected Poems, 1938
50 Poems, 1940
1 x 1 [One Times One], 1944
XAIPE: 71 Poems, 1950
Poems 1923–1954, 1954
95 Poems, 1958
100 Selected Poems, 1959
73 Poems, 1963

Complete Poems 1923–1962, 1972
Complete Poems 1904–1962, 1991

PROSE
The Enormous Room, 1922
Eimi [I Am], 1933
i: six nonlectures, 1953
Fairy Tales, 1965

OTHER WORKS
Him (play), 1927
CIOPW (artwork), 1931

INDEX

Published by Creative Education
123 South Broad Street, Mankato, Minnesota 56001
Creative Education is an imprint of The Creative Company
Copyright © 1994 Creative Education
International copyrights reserved in all countries.
No part of this book may be reproduced in any form without
written permission from the publisher.
Printed in Italy.
Art Direction: Rita Marshall
Designed by: Stephanie Blumenthal
Artwork by Stasys Eidrigevicius
Library of Congress Cataloging-in-Publication Data
Berry, S. L.
    E. E. Cummings / written by Skip L. Berry.
        p. cm. — (Voices in poetry)
    Includes bibliographical references and index.
    Summary: A biography of the twentieth-century American
writer whose poetry combined artistic composition with word play
and traditional rhyme and meter. Includes examples of his work.
    ISBN 0-88682-611-X
    1. Cummings, E. E. (Edward Estlin), 1894–1962—
Biography—Juvenile literature.   2. Poets, American—20th
century—Biography—Juvenile literature.   3. Young adult poetry,
American. [1. Cummings, E. E. (Edward Estlin), 1894–1962.
2. Poets, American.   3. American poetry.]   I. Title.   II. Series:
Voices in poetry (Mankato, Minn.)
PS3505.U334Z563   1993
811'.52—dc20   93-743
[B]   CIP
                                                                AC

9 8 7 6 5 4 3 2